Opening a New Catholic School:

A Series of Case Studies

Robert J. Kealey, Ed.D., Editor

Department of Elementary Schools
National Catholic Educational Association

ISBN 1-55833-189-1

Contents

List of Exhibits

Preface

During the last ten years, almost 200 new Catholic schools have opened across the country. These openings have occurred at the elementary, middle, and senior high school levels. This concrete demonstration of faith in Catholic schools attests to the deep belief that Catholic parents and other members of the Catholic community have in the quality of Catholic schools and to their desire to have schools that actively foster Christian values. The large number of phone calls that NCEA receives asking for advice on how to open new schools indicates that this trend will continue.

This renewed interest in building Catholic schools has led to the development of this book. When this project was originally envisioned, the editor had in mind to set down a step-by-step procedure on how to open a new school. After consulting with a number of people about this format, the editor quickly came to realize that no one procedure is possible. About as many routes to opening a new school exist as there are parish and school communities that have opened new schools. A decision was made, therefore, to present a series of case studies. This approach would be more practical for those contemplating opening a new school, since they could pick and choose from the various experiences those elements that would be most helpful to them.

The book contains nine case studies; some are very brief and direct, while others contain detailed directions and forms. Some schools began because of the initiative of the clergy; others began because of the determination of parents. Whatever the motivation, these are stories of faith.

This book was initiated by the NCEA Department of Elementary Schools with the support and assistance of the NCEA Department of Secondary Schools and the NCEA Department of Chief Administrators of Catholic Education. Tara McCallum, editorial assistant for the NCEA Department of Elementary Schools, edited the manuscript for its final presentation and oversaw all steps in its production. Tia Gray of the NCEA Communications Department designed the cover, and Beatriz Ruiz laid out the text of the book. The NCEA Department of Elementary

Schools Executive Committee expresses its gratitude to all of the above for their help with this important production.

As we stand at the doorway to the third millennium, the NCEA Department of Elementary Schools presents this book to the membership of NCEA with the hope that it will be a catalyst to impel other Catholic communities across the country to open other Catholic schools. This will help to achieve the 1990 vision of the American Catholic bishops of ensuring that Catholic schools are available for all Catholic parents who wish to send their children to them.

Kieran Hartigan, RSM   *Robert J. Kealey, Ed.D.*
President   *Executive Director*

NCEA Department of Elementary Schools
Easter, 1997

Procedures for Opening a New School

Diocese of Arlington, Virginia

Timothy J. McNiff, Ed.D., Superintendent of Schools

In light of the enrollment difficulties Catholic schools have experienced over the past two decades, the recent trend of opening new Catholic schools has certainly become a welcome challenge. The Diocese of Arlington has been fortunate in that the resurgence of applications to the Catholic schools in northern Virginia has necessitated the opening of six new schools in the past several years. This growth is complemented by plans for additional schools to be started at the rate of one per year for the remainder of the 1990s. Although credit for this increase can be attributed to many factors, paramount to this expansion is the unfledging support the Arlington Catholic Schools has received from the diocesan bishop and the local pastors.

The recent establishment of new schools in the Arlington diocese is the result of two separate forces at work: the addition of a new parish sponsoring a new school, and private schools (religious and/or lay owned) soliciting the diocesan bishop to be recognized as Catholic. These initiatives necessitated that a policy be produced by the Office of Catholic Schools to address the procedures for accepting new schools. Particularly important in this policy is the language that acknowledges the private Catholic schools. This policy and its guidelines are limited to the field of religious education, as required by canon law. They ensure the need to safeguard the canonical prerogatives of the diocesan bishop in the specific areas relating to religious education, while avoiding unwanted exposure to the diocese of liability issues relating to the autonomy of the private school. Although the legal considerations for the creation of a new school are part of the process, this chapter focuses on the logistical procedures for building new *diocesan* schools. Exhibit 1 at the end of the chapter is a model of the approval process the diocese developed.

Of the most recent schools that opened in the Arlington diocese, two resulted from transforming existing parish facilities into a school building. The other new schools (created in conjunction with a new parish) resemble the old Church model, whereby the new parish started with the construction of the school. Following are the procedural guidelines that supported the process of establishing these schools.

A. Documenting the Need for a New School

For reasons other than just ascertaining the need for a new school, the Arlington diocese conducted a demographic study to determine where the population growth was expanding. This document, in conjunction with the prevalence of waiting lists at neighboring Catholic schools, became the strongest indication a new school was needed. The Catholic schools office also tracked, although more anecdotal in nature, the number of inquiries expressing an interest in a new school in different regions of the diocese.

B. Addressing the Financial Considerations of a New School

Once there was consensus from a pastor and the Catholic schools office to explore the possibility of a new school, identifying the financial realities of building and annually supporting a school was the next step. Key members of the project (pastor, Office of Catholic Schools, and other chancery staff members) began to draft several budgets:

1. A three-year operating budget for the proposed school was done to determine the projected enrollment, tuition rates, parish subsidy, and salary expenses. The committee's analysis of these reports helped to channel a discussion on the possibility of funding a new school on a year-to-year basis. The Office of Catholic Schools, after referring to other schools in the diocese, affirmed the projections.

2. On the premise the operating budgets were acceptable, a second budget was created to address the capital requirements of a new school. The involvement (advisory only at the time) of an architect and/or contractor was very useful in identifying all of the construction and soft costs required to construct or renovate a building.

3. The capital budget also had to identify how the one-time expenses would be funded. If it was determined a debt would be incurred because the total expense in the capital budget could not be funded from a capital campaign or other fund-raisers, then the operating budget was reviewed to determine if the school's annual opera-

tions should absorb debt retirement via a monthly mortgage payment. Often the results of this stage determined the size of the new school. If the construction costs became too rich for the budget, the option of building a K-5 instead of K-8 school, with the understanding additional grades would be added in the future, was entertained.

C. Soliciting Diocesan Approval to Proceed

In the Arlington diocese, diocesan finance and construction committees serve as advisory panels for the bishop. These two structures help to ensure that proper planning is incorporated in all expansion projects. Prior to any new construction in excess of $10,000, all diocesan initiatives must secure the approval of these two committees and ultimately of the diocesan bishop. These committees listen to a presentation by the school representatives, who attempt to demonstrate the need for a new school, share the preliminary operating and capital budgets, and offer a rough sketch of the new building. It became imperative at this point in the process to demonstrate the support from the local pastors for the creation of a new school in their region of the diocese.

Although it varies according to the circumstances, the results of a parent survey are sometimes presented to the diocesan committees as evidence of the need to build a school. At other times, it is decided not to conduct such a survey until preliminary approval has been received. There is no formal policy in this regard. If a survey is utilized, however, it is politically important to articulate clearly the purpose of the survey and stress that responses to the questionnaire will not be interpreted as a commitment; rather, they will help to determine a possible need for a school.

D. Including Professionals in the Process

As the process continues to mature, it becomes necessary eventually to hire a team of professionals. Listed below are examples of how these individuals become influential.

1. If land for the new parish/school is required, the inclusion of real-estate professionals (e.g., attorneys, real-estate agents) to find and negotiate suitable land is necessary. Because of the unique nature of the Church and the benefits it offers the community, devoting time and resources to this part of the project is important. There are numerous opportunities to secure land at no cost or with significant reductions to the asking price. Including the right professionals to provide their expertise is immensely helpful in keeping costs to a minimum.

3

2. Once the right location is determined and a price is set, civil engineers need to conduct a feasibility study (an example of a soft cost to be included in the preliminary capital budget) to determine, among other details, if the land is viable for a new school. Zoning considerations, environmental concerns, traffic ordinances, and wetlands issues are examples of topics addressed within the feasibility study.

3. At this stage, the process of receiving bids from architects begins. Their presentations begin to identify some of the parameters of, and possibilities for, the new building. Once an architect is under contract, the finer details of how the new building will be constructed and the associated costs of the project take shape. For those new schools that will also serve as a parish facility, it is important for the preconstruction planning to be sensitive to the needs of the church. Converting classrooms to be used as parish offices, building an oversized gym that will accommodate Sunday liturgies, and creating space for a sacristy are requirements of the parish that must be addressed in the construction of the building. It is also advisable to inform the architect if the new building needs to be smaller than the size that will be required eventually (most times due to limited financing). Planning accommodations for future expansion will realize savings on future construction; for example, have cut-off valves for all utility lines installed at the location where it is anticipated the expansion will occur.

This stage is also the most opportune time to give "ownership" to the key people who will be called upon to make the new school a reality. While remaining advisory, parents and other individuals involved in the capital campaign should be allowed to provide input on various features for the new school.

4. During this time, plans for a fund-raising campaign begin. If it is determined that outside professional assistance is required (a decision that should not be made until an assessment is done of the size of the project and the in-house capabilities of the staff/volunteers), that search should include interviews of several firms. Though not always necessary, investment in a fund-raising feasibility study (to assess the potential for raising money) is sometimes prudent. In conjunction with the parish involvement, it is strongly recommended that a "community" capital campaign be created to help raise additional money separate from the funds from a parish or diocese.

E. Receiving Final Diocesan Approval

With greater detail about the project now available, the project is again presented to the bishop (via the two committees) for final

4

approval. At these meetings, refinements to the financing of the project, a construction calendar, and miscellaneous items are discussed. The Arlington diocese has a policy whereby all excess assets of the parishes are used to fund an "internal bank." This in-house resource, known as the Diocesan Investment and Loan Program, lends money to approved diocesan projects (standard terms are usually 6.5 percent over 7 years) with the provision that 40 percent of the construction costs has been raised.

Should outside financing from a commercial lender be required, a team of loan officers assists the project in procuring the best-possible mortgage arrangements. Again, all of the soft costs involved in mortgage financing, such as interest on construction draws, need to be captured in the project's capital budget.

F. Beginning Construction

During the actual construction period, several activities continue. The fund-raising efforts certainly become a way of life. The architect, along with the diocesan construction management team, provides regular monitoring of the construction progress.

This is also when the nonconstruction elements for a new school kick into high gear. The Office of Catholic Schools begins a search for a school principal and staff. Curriculum details and school policies are finalized. The marketing of the new school for recruitment purposes and the procedures for registration are addressed. After the administration and staff are hired, the Office of Catholic Schools administers in-service programs for the staff.

As with most endeavors that are of the magnitude of a new school, proper planning and a great deal of patience are necessary. The business of construction, the budgeting of finances, and the building of a "small city" of school children bring many challenges. The antidote for those obstacles must be the constant reminder that the project *will succeed* and with it will come the reality that more children will continue to be educated under the guidance of our first teacher, Jesus. That accomplishment will far surpass the trials realized during the process.

Exhibit 1

Approval Process for Opening
a New Catholic School

Rationale

All schools designated as Catholic must follow the policies and guidelines authorized by the diocesan bishop regarding religious education, catechists, and liturgy. Catholic-designated schools operated by entities of the Diocese of Arlington must also meet additional standards relating to academic excellence and financial viability. The process of approving and operating Catholic schools in the diocese should take into account the varying requirements for schools, depending upon their ownership and whether they are diocesan schools or independent schools administered by a religious community or lay corporation.

Policy

Diocesan Schools Sponsored by the Diocese or Parish. Before a parish or group of parishes seeks the bishop's written approval to open a diocesan school, the pastor or pastors must first:

1. Provide written notification to both the bishop and the superintendent of schools of the desire to open a school.

2. Acknowledge that he/they have reviewed and will comply with the publication *Policies and Guidelines: Catholic Schools, Diocese of Arlington.*

3. Seek a recommendation for approval from the diocesan school board, based on its assessment of the proven need for, or evident utility of, a Catholic school in that particular geographic area of the diocese. Data provided to the school board shall include estimates of student enrollment, opinions of surrounding pastors, and projected operating budgets for the future school.

4. Seek a recommendation of approval from the diocesan finance committee, based on its assessment of the proven ability of the parish to fund the construction in accordance with the relevant sections of the diocesan handbook and cost-effective operation of the school over the long term.

5. Provide adequate evidence to the secretary for religious education/director of the diocesan office of catechetics, based upon the parish(es) performance in its existing children's catechetics programs, that the requirements set forth in the relevant sections of the diocesan handbook on religious education will be met.

6. Provide additional information, as may be requested, to the board of consultors if further consultation is warranted.

Independent Schools Sponsored by a Religious Community or Lay Corporation. Consistent with Canon 803 of the *Code of Canon Law*, written approval from the diocesan bishop must be obtained before a school may be designated as a Catholic school. A non-diocesan school seeking the designation of Catholic shall have its materials reviewed by the secretary for religious education and by the diocesan school board, who will forward to the diocesan bishop their recommendations on the appropriateness of the school being designated Catholic.

Before an independent school may be designated as a Catholic school, the owners and administrators of the school must first:

1. Provide written notification to the diocesan bishop and the Office of Catholic Education of their desire to operate a Catholic school that would be sponsored by either a religious community or a lay corporation. Incorporated in this notification must be a sworn statement that the owners and administrators of the school agree to safeguard the canonical prerogatives of the diocesan bishop in the specific areas of religious education, selection of religion textbooks, fitness of religion teachers, spiritual direction, and liturgical norms.

2. Provide letters of recommendation from the pastor(s) of the parish(es) in which the school is located and from the pastor(s) of the owners and chief administrator of the school. If the school is moving from another diocese, a letter of endorsement from the episcopal vicar for religious education and from the superintendent of schools of that diocese are also required.

3. Include in the governing charter of the organization the affirmation to safeguard the canonical prerogatives of the diocesan bishop as stated in the notification referred to in item 1 above. A copy of the organization's charter must be submitted with the referenced notification.

4. Provide evidence satisfactory to the Office of Catholic Education that the school has been in existence and operating for a minimum of five years.

5. Participate in a candidacy period (minimum of two years), starting with the commencement of the school year following submittal of the application, before seeking the formal designation of Catholic for the school. The candidacy period of a school's application will extend until that school's process of adding any additional grades is

completed. During the candidacy period, the school will provide to the Office of Catholic Education—

a. A school philosophy/mission statement that is consistent with the principles of Catholic education enunciated in the Church documents *To Teach as Jesus Did* (1973), *The Catholic School (1977)*, and *The Religious Dimensions of Education in a Catholic School* (1988)

b. Evidence that the school is following the religious education guidelines of the diocese by—

- Employing religion teachers who meet diocesan standards for catechists (i.e., have catechist certification, have a proper grasp of Church doctrine, are a witness of the Christian life, and exhibit the art of teaching) and who are certified diocesan catechists
- Explaining the religious education program of the school to parents at regular intervals

c. Evidence that the school has obtained, or will work towards, accreditation by the Virginia Catholic Education Association (VCEA) and/or diocesan-deemed equivalent for schools

d. A written description of the structure, goals, and governance of the school, including identification of, and biographic information about, the persons responsible for the governance of the school

e. An agreement to operate the school during the candidacy period in facilities not owned by the Diocese of Arlington or its parishes

6. Also provide to the Office of Catholic Education during the candidacy period and annually thereafter—

a. A current list of all administrators and faculty members who supervise and/or teach religion education, including their professional assignment.

b. A current list of textbooks being used. High schools must also provide copies of all religion texts.

c. Copies of all handbooks and policy manuals used by the school.

d. Statistical data completed on the form requested by the National Catholic Educational Association.

e. A current list of members of the governing board. A minimum of 50 percent of board members must be practicing Catholics.

Upon receiving the designation of Catholic, independent private schools are eligible to request by written application to the Office of Catholic Education participation in all educational programs developed for schools or sponsored by the diocese.

The Opening of St. John Neumann Regional Catholic School

Archdiocese of Atlanta, Georgia

Sister Dawn Gear, GNSH, M.Ed., Principal

In 1980, a task force was formed by the Archdiocese of Atlanta to study the needs of Gwinnett County, an area with no Catholic schools. With a rapidly growing suburban population, there was a great demand for Catholic education. A survey gave credence to this need. The proposed site for a regional school was on the grounds of St. John Neumann Church, a newly established parish. The issues raised were (a) how to allocate costs between tuition, parish subsidy, and the archdiocese for capital costs and school operations and (b) how to maintain affordable tuition for the average family within the region.

In 1981, St. John Neumann Parish submitted a proposal to the Atlanta archdiocese to build 18 classrooms for religious education. The archdiocese was faced with the decision of approving the project as submitted and waiting to construct a new school or constructing a new school, with little guarantees, that could be used also for parish religious education classes. The finance committee, acting on the concept of a shared facility for religious education and a future Catholic school, studied the cost of constructing 18 classrooms to meet the Southern Association of Colleges and Schools (SACS) standards. The final cost would be 50 percent above the initial cost proposed by the parish to meet SACS requirements.

The archdiocesan finance office suggested the following: that 18 classrooms would be constructed to SACS specification. St. John Neumann Parish would pay the original cost of the religious education classrooms only, and the archdiocese would loan the future new school the balance. The parish had permission to proceed immediately, while a new school would be delayed. The latter would be a regional school serving seven parishes. The tuition would break even for operational expenses. A loan would be made to finance the original amount to meet SACS standards as well as the future construction costs, including construction of a cafeteria, gym, library, additional classrooms, and school offices. The archdiocesan loan divided by the number of students would be the per-child subsidy paid by the parish that the child attended in the region. Thus, over $3 million would be saved using a shared-facility concept in conjunction with parish needs and initiating construction at an earlier date to avoid later inflationary construction costs.

The St. John Neumann Regional Catholic School was founded by the late Archbishop Thomas A. Donnellan in 1986, two years prior to the estimated opening date of 1988. On the opening day, 160 students were registered. Some operating subsidy was necessary in the early years, and it was added to the capital debt, which will be fully amortized in the year 2005. By 1990, the school was self-sufficient with a balanced budget. The original 7 parishes soon increased to 13 due to the school's excellent reputation.

After the financing was settled, a school board was established, with representation from the original 7 parishes. Its first point of business was to search for a principal; a religious sister was hired. She began working in January 1986, with many tasks to accomplish. Between January and August, school finances were set up, a secretary was hired, and equipment was purchased. An assessment was made to take into account the needs of the future student body. The admissions policy and procedures were written, the curriculum was adopted, and textbooks were purchased with the advice and counsel of peer principals in the archdiocese.

Preparation for an open house in the spring included preparation of an admissions packet, newspaper articles, and church bulletin announcements. The open house was successful, and interested parents applied for admission. Testing, evaluation of applications with teacher references, and standardized testing results ensued during the next month. Experienced teachers were approached to assist in the final evaluation and acceptance of students.

The principal advertised for teachers. This was followed by interviews and hiring the most qualified. During the summer, a "Happy Birthday, St. John Neumann" party took place, and the prospective students, parents, and teachers came to celebrate the "birth" of a new school. With the assistance of another religious sister who came to St. John Neumann School in June, the principal launched more projects: writing a preliminary philosophy and objectives as well as the faculty and parent handbooks. Consultation with the surrounding Catholic schools helped to formulate these items, which were later accepted and endorsed by the new board, new faculty, and new parents to the school.

The administrator hired a maintenance person to get the original religious education building ready for the opening of school—a lounge and workroom, restrooms, and all the necessary purchases for each classroom were taken care of. With only four people on board during the summer months, the principal looked forward to August 1986, when St. John Neumann School would open its doors to 160 students and 9 teachers, including a physical education teacher and a volunteer music teacher.

Two weeks after school opened, Archbishop Donnellan officiated at a liturgy and groundbreaking ceremony for the construction of a new gym, library, cafeteria, additional classrooms, and art, music, and science labs. The dedication of the new buildings took place in April 1988. The principal immediately established ties with, and a strong commitment among, all members of the school community. From the very beginning, a large number of interested and talented people came to the rescue and helped in many areas: organizing a home and school association, choosing a school uniform, and volunteering for numerous jobs. Realizing that the tuition could not possibly cover many of the extra items a good school needs, the parents joined the principal in establishing some fund-raisers. During the 1986-1987 school year, playground equipment was purchased. In 1987-1988, a computer lab with 25 computers was in place.

With the archdiocese contracting Catholic Schools Management for All Catholic Schools, St. John Neumann School benefitted from this assistance and launched a development program. A director of development was hired for the school in 1987, and new ideas came forward to raise sufficient funds for numerous projects. In 1989, an annual fund was established, and funds were earmarked to improve the library. The

11

school worked on obtaining sufficient books to qualify for SACS initial accreditation. A certified media specialist, with the help of many volunteers, catalogued more than enough books to meet SACS standards for the initial accreditation in 1990, and by 1994, the library was completely computerized for the SACS interim review.

Every year, new goals were set in motion. Some of these goals included new textbooks; library and audiovisual equipment; materials for science, math, and social studies; new programs for primary grades; and additional computers. In the summer of 1995, an expansion program took place which involved enlarging the media center, a resource center for children with learning disabilities, a faculty professional room, a conference room, admissions, development and finance offices. In the past ten years, the school has raised almost a million dollars through its development and fund-raising programs.

Every year, registration increased, and by 1990, there were three sections for kindergarten and first and second grades and two sections for third through eighth grades. The initial accreditation for SACS was also accomplished in 1990.

In 1994, the enrollment reached 600 students. Also in that year, St. John Neumann Regional School became a U.S. Department of Education Blue Ribbon School of Excellence. In 1995, the interim interview for SACS was completed. The school now employs a staff of 64, which include a principal and an assistant principal; certified classroom teachers; art, music, physical education, and computer teachers; instructional aides; a media specialist; a guidance counselor; a curriculum director; and maintenance and cafeteria personnel.

The school has been the recipient of many blessings. Its strength has come from a faith-filled community that lives the gospel values and provides its students with a wholesome Christian environment for learning.

Opening a new school is certainly a challenge. God led this school's principal to move on to open school number 2. The rewards are plentiful, and with them come a spiritual promise of a "high place in heaven!"

Charlotte Catholic High School: The Miracle on Highway 51

Diocese of Charlotte, North Carolina

Michael F. Skube, Ph.D.,
Superintendent of Schools

The roots of Catholic secondary education in Charlotte, North Carolina, took hold in 1887 with the founding of St. Mary's Seminary, located in the downtown area and staffed by the Sisters of Mercy. Sixteen years later, the O'Donoghue School—named in honor of Dr. Denis O'Donoghue, a Charlotte physician and major contributor to the school building—was constructed nearby.

In 1929, a new O'Donoghue School was built, with the Sisters of Mercy retaining responsibility for Catholic secondary education in Charlotte. The first high school class, of five girls, graduated in 1946, and in 1948, the O'Donoghue High School was accredited by the Southern Association of Colleges and Schools. When the need for a larger, more centrally located facility arose, a new building was constructed south of the downtown area in Charlotte. Soon afterwards, the school became known as Charlotte Catholic High School (CCHS).

With the beginning of the 1992-1993 school year, the Catholic Schools of Charlotte began operation as a regionalized school system with five elementary schools and Charlotte Catholic High School. Three of the five elementary schools were new schools. Two of the new schools were larger, expanded facilities that replaced schools that were closed. The other new elementary school that opened had a capacity of 600 students. With the beginning of the 1993-1994 school year, the total enrollment of the schools increased by 32 percent, for a total of 2,900 students.

As the students in the elementary schools move towards graduation, most of these young people will want to continue on to CCHS. In 1993-1994, however, CCHS was overcrowded. Feasibility-study interviews and focus groups indicated that the major weakness with CCHS was its facilities. Something had to be done.

After extensive research, the Diocese of Charlotte identified and purchased the former Stearns Catalytic building on Highway 51. The award-winning architectural firm of Little and Associates and a general contractor, Whelchel and Associates, were hired to work with Sr. Paulette Williams, principal of CCHS, and her staff to make a vacant office building into a state-of-the-art educational facility and, at the same time, save millions of dollars!

The former Stearns Catalytic building, with 119,000 square feet of usable space, was renovated to include classroom space, Our Lady of Mercy Chapel, an expansive new kitchen and cafeteria, and a media center that houses a state-of-the-art integrated communications system that networks all school telephone, computer, intercom, and audiovisual systems. The assessed valuation of the facility and property was in excess of $4 million, with the purchase price being $2 million.

An additional 39,000-square foot building was constructed on the site to house a gymnasium, a fine-arts facility, and additional classrooms. The 1,400-seat gymnasium facility includes a spacious stage for fine-arts productions, a choral room, band room, weight room, wrestling room, and six locker rooms for physical education classes and sports teams. The new academic facilities will accommodate 1,200 students. Located on 14.5 acres of land, the site had sufficient space for a new football/soccer stadium and over 400 parking spaces. The stadium seats 3,000 and is complete with a press box, concession building, and restroom facilities.

The projected cost of the facility and land purchase; renovation of the present facility; and construction of the gym, stadium, and parking lots was $10 million.

Comparable facilities were being built in the public sector for $18 million. Realizing the need for a larger high school and millions of dollars of savings with this opportunity, the pastors, parishioners, and community people came together, under the guidance of Jim Kelley, the diocesan director of development, for a very successful capital campaign. Under the dynamic leadership of our spiritual leader of the diocese, Bishop William G. Curlin, friends, parents, alumni, and the community met the campaign goal of raising $3 million. The Diocese of Charlotte committed a $7 million loan to help meet the total cost.

With the opening of the new high school, there was an opportunity to use the former high school building. After three years of planning, school year 1995-1996 began not only with the opening of the new high school facility but also with the opening of the former high school as a middle school with 737 sixth-, seventh-, and eighth-grade students attending. Because families may have students in three separate facilities, a bus transportation program was put in place serving 350 students.

Bishop William G. Curlin and Father Mauricio West, chancellor, are to be commended for their continuing support of Catholic school education. In addition, with the switch from a K-8 grade setting to a K-5 grade setting at the elementary schools; the addition of a middle school and the opening of a new high school campus; and the initiation of a new school-bus system, the faculty and staff at all seven schools deserve much praise for making the transition a smooth one for all involved.

Serra Catholic Elementary School

Diocese of Orange, California

Brother William Carriere, FSC, Ph.D., Superintendent
Audrey Tellers, M.Ed., Principal

S erra Catholic Elementary School began in September 1995 under the direction of three parishes. It opened with grades K-6, some classes having two sections of each grade, and an enrollment of 250 students.

As early as 1992, families that had moved into a very high growth area of south Orange County quickly realized that there was no Catholic elementary school. Although a large Catholic high school had opened in the area in 1987, there seemed to be no movement to develop an elementary school, even with the sizable growth in a population with small children. In 1993, some strong efforts were made among a number of families that hoped for a school to open in September 1994. Late in the spring of 1994, an initial survey was sent out to parishioners in three parishes, and the overwhelming support from the survey indicated that a school should open in the fall of 1995.

A central committee was formed that included members of the three parish communities. The purpose of this committee was to represent the interests of the three parishes. It would be responsible for making the necessary contacts with diocesan officials from the Catholic schools, construction, and finance departments to assure that all diocesan guidelines were followed and for keeping the bishop well informed of the progress, as ultimately his approval would be needed.

At the time of the initial proposal, there was a piece of land available that would be able to accommodate a temporary school site and a permanent one. Because it was necessary to act quickly on this

17

possibility, since obtaining land in this area was particularly difficult, the committee stressed the necessity of obtaining a lease as soon as possible. This helped to drive the whole work of establishing the school by 1995. It is important to note here that one of the three parishes was brand new and in the middle of its own building project for a church. There was some real concern as to whether the people of that parish could afford to take on other pledges for a school at that time, but the energy of the people clearly indicated a willingness to take on this project also. The other two parishes also had some building projects of their own but none as large as constructing a new church.

The new school would serve the needs of three parishes: San Francisco Solano, Santiago de Compostela, and St. Kilian. In several meetings with the three pastors, the superintendent of Catholic schools, and the associate superintendent, the guidelines for the school were established. The school would be tri-sponsored, and issues of authority, responsibility, accountability, and ownership would have to be re-solved. Exhibit 5 at the end of this chapter is a model working draft of the joint-sponsored agreement.

Before any of this could be developed, however, the bishop asked for a financial feasibility study to see if the project could be supported by the parishes. The survey included questions that asked families what they could afford in tuition and what funds could be raised through donors and gifts not only from the families themselves, but also from people in the parishes who were interested in supporting the school. This study was important, as it would help to determine the bishop's approval. (See Exhibits 2 and 3 at the end of this chapter for adapta-tions of the questionnaire and the grade summary report.)

It was decided from the beginning that the school would open with grades K-6, with some grades doubled to serve the expected population of the school in the first year. The financial feasibility study proved that even more money would be necessary to open the school, so the committee and a number of other interested parties looked for more ways to obtain funds. Early voluntary, unsolicited contributions in the amount of $177,000 from 126 families and other pledges would help the initial funding of building plans, land leasing, and so forth. Setting the tuition and fee rates that families were willing to pay also helped to provide the bishop with the necessary financial picture to begin the school.

In December 1994, parents were notified of the progress of school development. Pledges were sought and an initial enrollment form was sent to all families in the three parishes. Also, these first families were asked to give an additional amount of money as a gift to assist in the initial fund-raising effort. Early registration in January 1995 with a collection of fees would also provide needed funding. Some families contributed advance tuition. At this point, the committee was able to develop a good cash flow. With over $400,000 at hand and the design of two major fund-raising events to be conducted in the spring and summer of 1995, much was in order for the meeting with the bishop. A blue ribbon committee was formed to be responsible for all of the fund-raising from this point on in the development of the school.

There were several planned meetings to settle other issues. The admissions policy was set (Exhibit 4 at the end of this chapter is a model of it). Incoming students and their families had to be active members of one of the three parishes. "Active parishioner" meant regular attendance at mass, use of the parish envelope, and involvement in parish activities. No one from outside the parishes would be admitted at this time; therefore, parents would need a letter from their pastor as part of the admissions process. It was further decided that one third of the school population would come from each parish. The details of that decision would be worked out on a family basis in order to keep families together as much as possible. This arrangement would change each year, according to the experience of the number of students available at each grade level in each of the parishes.

One pastor would serve as the liaison between the pastors and the school administration for a specified term. The pastor of the school would serve a three-year term and be an ex-officio member of the consultative school board. He would be responsible for contacting the other pastors, especially when decisions required their involvement. Decisions of the three pastors would be communicated by the lead pastor to the principal. In most cases, the principal would be involved with the three pastors in executive sessions, and the principal and lead pastor would meet on a weekly basis.

Sacramental preparation of all the students would take place within the parishes' programs. It was decided early that portable units would be used for classrooms, administration offices, multipurpose rooms, and other needed areas for clerical help and storage. An action timeline was designed; for a sample, see Exhibit 6 at the end of this chapter. Although the timeline was changed a number of times because of further research required by the bishop, it was very useful for helping everyone to handle their individual and group responsibilities.

In March 1995, the meeting with the bishop took place to formally approve the opening of the school. The school was approved with definitive guidelines regarding the purchase of the land, the responsibility of the three pastors, and the ownership of the school by the parishes. At this point, a search began for the principal. As it was very late in the spring, the associate superintendent became the acting principal so registration of students and the interviewing and hiring of faculty could begin.

Between March and June of 1995, student registration, faculty interviewing and hiring, and the acquisition of the modular units took place. The central committee was fortunate enough to receive a large donation of modular units because a major firm closed its plant and had the units available. As they were in good condition, the units were easy to set up within a reasonable amount of time. Registrations were excellent, and clearly there would be enough students to populate the school for its first year. Some families had decided to wait until the school was in operation for one year before enrolling their children. In other cases, because of the late timeline for the approval of the school, some families had to return to their former school because registration was due before the new school was approved and they did not want to lose their place. It should be noted that it is critical that the timeline for the approval of the school is set early enough so that parents can choose to send their children to the new school without any risks.

Three candidates emerged for principalship. The principal chosen had a good history of administration in Catholic elementary schools and also had been the superintendent of Catholic schools in another diocese. We had required that applicants for principalship at the new school have a minimum of five years as a principal in Catholic schools, with a proven record of success as an administrator. In our minds that meant strong leadership qualities as a spiritual and academic leader. It would have been more helpful to the diocesan office if the principal could have been hired one year before the school's opening so he or she could have formed the committees to do all of the preparatory work well in advance.

Once the new principal was hired, she began working with the pastors and the committees. Registrations continued to go well, and several committees of parents went to work on such items as uniforms, classroom furniture, development of a first-year handbook, playground development, work with city officials, and continued dialogue with the diocese. Again, we were faced with a very short timeline for getting under way; long hours were spent throughout the spring and summer. Budgets were adjusted as more money became available.

During the summer of 1995, a major gathering was held to allow parents to meet each other and to meet the new principal and many of the faculty who had been hired during the spring. The gathering was a mini-fiesta with game and food booths, and it was a wonderful fund-raiser. Since we were on the site of the school, all had an opportunity to see the modular units that were about to be set up.

It took the majority of the summer to set up the units. Furniture had been ordered, and one of the units was set up early as the office so that school business could be done while construction continued. Although it looked as if much of the preparation would not be ready for the opening, the opposite was true. Finishing touches were being completed right up to the day before school began. The teachers were great, arriving at the site early to assist. Parents were on call to help in any way that the principal needed. It was a heavy, concentrated summer.

The doors opened the first week in September with an assembly at which diocesan representatives were on hand to welcome the parents and students. There were 250 students on the playground. The enthusiasm was overwhelming. People were so proud of the fact that actually within eight months we had the beginnings of a very fine school. Dedication day was set for October 4, 1995, the feast of St. Francis and the principal's birthday.

The school is now in its second year, with double the enrollment. It is projected that the school will maintain a population of approximately 1,000 students. All look forward to the building of the permanent buildings. It is exceptional to note that the school, in its modular buildings, houses a science lab, a state-of-the-art computer lab, a learning center, a multipurpose room, and classrooms for three prekindergartens, three kindergartens, and grades 1-7.

Everyone strongly believes that through the efforts of parents who were determined to have a Catholic elementary school in their region, Serra Catholic Elementary was born. Without their very hard work, it is unlikely that there would have been such great success in so short a time.

Exhibit 2

Preliminary Survey of Parishioners

Dear Parishioners:

A grassroots effort by parents interested in establishing a regional Catholic elementary school in this community has been gaining momentum. To ensure that this effort conforms to diocesan requirements, we have been receiving guidance and direction from Brother William Carriere, FSC, the diocesan superintendent of schools.

As envisioned, a regional diocesan Catholic school would accommodate Catholic children from the three parishes of this area: Santiago de Compostela in Lake Forest, St. Kilian in Mission Viejo, and San Francisco Solano in Rancho Santa Margarita. The school would teach and model our Roman Catholic faith, and active parish participation (including sacramental preparation and celebrations) would be normative. The pastors of each of the parishes have authorized this survey.

The information gathered through this survey is essential to determining the need for, and scope of, such a school. Your timely response is crucial to the development of this process. We ask that you complete the survey and return it in the envelope provided by [*insert date*].

Any questions or additional comments may be directed to the following core group of parents:

[*List parents' names and telephone numbers.*]

In Christ's service,

Parents for Catholic Education

Regional Catholic Elementary School Questionnaire

1. How valuable do you feel a Catholic school education would be to the **spiritual formation** of the children of this area? (Please circle the number of the response that best matches the way you feel.)

Not very important	Somewhat important	Very important

1   2   3   4   5

2. How valuable do you feel a Catholic school education would be to the **character development** of the children of this area?

1   2   3   4   5

3. How valuable do you feel a Catholic school education would be to the **academic development** of the children of this area?

      1   2   3   4   5

4. Please indicate below, by placing a circle around the correct response, which grade level(s) your child(ren) will be entering in the September 1995 school year. Also, and most important, please indicate with a yes or no whether you would enroll your child(ren) in a new regional Catholic school at that time.

Child #1	yes	no	Pre-K	K	1	2	3	4	5	6	7	8
Child #2	yes	no	Pre-K	K	1	2	3	4	5	6	7	8
Child #3	yes	no	Pre-K	K	1	2	3	4	5	6	7	8
Child #4	yes	no	Pre-K	K	1	2	3	4	5	6	7	8
Child #5	yes	no	Pre-K	K	1	2	3	4	5	6	7	8
Child #6	yes	no	Pre-K	K	1	2	3	4	5	6	7	8
Child #7	yes	no	Pre-K	K	1	2	3	4	5	6	7	8
Child #8	yes	no	Pre-K	K	1	2	3	4	5	6	7	8
Child #9	yes	no	Pre-K	K	1	2	3	4	5	6	7	8
Child #10	yes	no	Pre-K	K	1	2	3	4	5	6	7	8

5. Please list the ages of any of your other children younger than prekindergarten age whom you would desire to send to a regional Catholic school in the future.

_____   _____   _____   _____   _____

6. Regarding the prekindergarten, which program would you be interested in?

    ❑ Half-day   ❑ Full-day

7. The real cost of educating each child must be the basis for establishing tuition. Please review the actual fees charged at Catholic and other religious elementary schools in this area:

St. Ann's (Christian)	$3,350
St. Edward's (Roman Catholic)	$2,600
St. John's (Episcopal)	$4,150
St. Margaret's (Episcopal)	$6,600
Mission Hills Christian School	$3,375

If you would consider enrolling one or more of your children in prekindergarten to eighth grade, please circle the highest tuition that you would be willing to pay. Keep in mind that we would strive to keep tuition as low as possible.

$2,600 $2,900 $3,200 $3,500 $3,800 $4100

8. Considering your own background and the advantage of a Catholic education (if applicable), please check the position(s) below to which you would be willing to contribute your time and talents to become part of making this vision a reality.

- ❑ Office assistant
- ❑ Classroom aide
- ❑ Physical education assistant
- ❑ Field-trip assistant
- ❑ Careers day participant
- ❑ Special-interest short-course teacher
- ❑ Retreat volunteer

Starting a school is an involved process. Many have volunteered their time and talent. Do you have any areas of expertise that might contribute to our effort?

_____

_____

_____

_____

9. Circle the mileage range from your location to the location of the new regional Catholic school that represents the farthest distance you would be willing to drive.

1-3 miles   4-6 miles   7-10 miles   10+ miles

10. Catholic schools have given many of us so much. You may have been so affected. You may have a current need for Catholic schooling, or you may have already educated your children. Many families of varying circumstances have indicated a desire to contribute to this effort.

As a parishioner of this parish, would you be willing to pledge to the permanent building fund?

❏ yes   ❏ no   ❏ undecided

11. (Optional) Please estimate the amount your pledge would be.

$_____

12. If you would like to be contacted now regarding this pledge, please initial here: _____.

13. Please refer to the map of the area included with this survey and indicate on the line below the coordinates of the area of your residence. (For example, Santa Margarita Catholic High School is within coordinate I-5.)

_____

14. Please write on the following lines any comments or suggestions you have.

_____

_____

_____

_____

Thank you sincerely for your time and effort.

(Please print)

Name:_____

Address:_____

City: _____ Zip Code:_____

Telephone:_____

Your Signature:_____

Exhibit 3

Results of the Preliminary Survey of Parishioners:
Projected Grade Summary Report

Grade	Students
Pre-K	287
K	208
1	183
2	153
3	134
4	138
5	121
6	109
7	99
8	40

Total students: 1,472

Exhibit 4

Catholic Elementary School Student Selection
Criteria and Guidelines

1. Student must be a registered Catholic and give name of his or her parish.
2. Students will be selected on a first-come, first-served basis.
3. Student must have parish involvement or a letter from the pastor and prior Catholic school support (scale from 1 to 5).
4. The number of accepted students from each of the three parishes should be approximately one third of the school population.
5. Families with additional children applying will receive preference for those additional children (in an effort to keep a family together).
6. There will be a standardized test/entrance exam.
7. Interview should be conducted with parents and the child.
8. Parents should submit a letter indicating the reason they want their child(ren) to attend a Catholic regional school.
9. A waiting list should be established based on the applicants' successful fulfillment of the above criteria.

Exhibit 5

Working Draft of the Joint-Sponsorship Agreement

Joint sponsorship of the regional Catholic elementary school is an agreement with St. Kilian, San Francisco Solano, and Santiago de Compostela parishes in the Diocese of Orange to have the regional school as an integral part of the educational ministry of the three parishes. The parishes commit themselves to provide the necessary leadership and support to ensure the continuation of the regional school within the jurisdiction of the parishes, the diocese, and the Department of Catholic Schools.

1. The pastors of the sponsoring parishes, in conjunction with the Department of Religious Education and the Department of Catholic Schools, will be responsible for ensuring that the religious education program, liturgical services, and sacramental preparation are in accord with diocesan and parish guidelines and policies.
2. The pastors and delegated priests will be responsible for the celebration of the Eucharist and the pastoral ministry to the students.
3. The pastors and associate priests shall visit the school and participate in appropriate school activities, as agreed upon with the principal.
4. The pastors, with the superintendent/associate superintendent of schools, have oversight of:
   - Selection of the principal according to the guidelines set by the Department of Catholic Schools
   - Supervision and approval of the budget
   - Approval of capital expenses according to the constructs of the responsibilities of the board in this area and diocesan guidelines
   - Approval of policies in the areas of board responsibilities (as outlined in the board constitution)
5. The pastors will evaluate the principal each year with the superintendent or associate superintendent and within the format used in the Department of Catholic Schools.
6. The pastors will meet annually with the superintendent and the associate superintendent to discuss all facets of the school, in an ongoing effort to ensure the religious formation of the school community and the quality of the academic program.
7. The pastors and the superintendent/associate superintendent will meet with the board annually to review its activities/responsibilities, its constitution, and its bylaws.

Exhibit 6

Action Timeline

(Note: There was a separate schedule for land and building development.)

December
Bishop's approval and announcement
Principal selection process begins
Development advisory council (DAC) meeting (delegation of duties
    by 12/15)
Registration letter sent to positive survey respondents (12/5)
Telephone/contact contributors
School masthead and logo designed
Registration packets assembled
Bishop's school committee meeting
School board selected
Pledge collection begins

January
Registration packets mailed
DAC committee meeting
Blue ribbon committee meeting/planning
Returned registration packets organized
Principal hired
General contractor proposals
School board meeting

February
Applicant testing begins
Teacher and staff recruitment begins
Registrants accepted
DAC committee meeting
Blue ribbon committee meeting
Textbook selection begins
General contractor/Modular-unit bidding
Teacher contracts signed
Liability insurance secured
School board meeting

March
Registration completed
Teacher contracts signed
School books ordered
Computer center planned
DAC committee meeting
Blue ribbon committee meeting

April
Fund-raiser
DAC committee meeting
Blue ribbon committee meeting
School board meeting

May
Construction begins
Phone system ordered
School desks, chairs, and equipment ordered
DAC committee meeting
Blue ribbon committee meeting
School board meeting

June
Advance tuition collected
Library books ordered
Office furniture ordered
Fund-raiser
Teacher staff meeting
DAC committee meeting
Blue ribbon committee meeting
School board meeting

July
Office equipment ordered
Educational aids ordered
Bookshelves ordered
Office computer ordered
Library computer and software ordered
Chalkboards ordered
Teacher staff meeting
DAC committee meeting

Blue ribbon committee meeting
School board meeting

August
Buildings completed
Computer center installed
Audiovisual equipment ordered
Landscaping completed
Classrooms prepared
Classroom books distributed
DAC committee meeting
Blue ribbon committee meeting
School board meeting

Fulfilling the Promise and the Dream: Annunciation Catholic Academy

Diocese of Orlando, Florida

Margaret E. Curran, Ed.D., Principal

D ue to the remarkable growth of the Catholic population in the state of Florida, the Diocese of Orlando has been experiencing an unparalleled interest in Catholic schools. For the past six years, most of the 27 elementary schools within the diocese have had extensive waiting lists. Forty-three of the 70 parishes in the diocese have never had schools, and as demand became greater, the existing schools were unable to adequately meet the needs of the neighboring parishes.

In February of 1995, Reverend Patrick J. Caverly, V.G., pastor of the Church of the Annunciation, met with a group of his parishioners to determine if the parish was ready and willing to take on the challenge of starting a new school. Their response was so positive and enthusiastic that "The Promise and the Dream" of founding Annunciation Catholic Academy was begun. An advisory board was formed and the project was inaugurated immediately. A formal needs assessment was not conducted because waiting lists for the neighboring Catholic schools were extensive, and local and diocesan officials agreed that taking time to statistically prove the obvious would only slow the project down.

Richard SanGiovanni, a parishioner, was hired as architect in February of 1995. For the next few months, he and key members of the

31

advisory board visited other schools and spoke to Father Caverly about concepts that were important to him. In addition, these extremely committed parish leaders read literature about trends in elementary education and spoke with educational leaders from the community before preparing initial plans.

The advisory board worked with Father Caverly throughout the spring of 1995. The principal of a neighboring Catholic school was added to the advisory board in April, and she worked with it on most phases of the project. The mission and philosophy of the school were determined early in the spring so that all subsequent decisions could be made in light of what had been decided as the parish's vision for the school.

The parish's response to the project was overwhelming. Two kindergarten classes were started in leased modular classrooms in the fall of 1995. Projections were to add a first grade in the fall of 1996 while fund-raising and building plans were finalized for the school, which eventually would become kindergarten to grade 8 in structure. Even though there were 1,200 students in the parish's excellent religious education program, the momentum that would eventually build was never anticipated.

As the fund-raising phase of "The Promise and the Dream" began in the fall of 1995, it became apparent that the parish was willing to make a serious financial commitment to the project. It was equally apparent that the parish wanted a full K-8 school as soon as possible. Given the enormous amount of support, it was decided to open a full elementary school in the fall of 1996. A principal was selected by Father Caverly at the beginning of October of 1995, and in December she began working at Annunciation two days a week while continuing her duties as principal of a neighboring Catholic school the other three days. The official groundbreaking ceremony was held with Bishop Norbert M. Dorsey, C.P., on December 16, 1995. A stated campaign goal of $5 million for the construction of the school and renovation of the church was reached before the end of December 1995.

During early January 1996, three orientation sessions were held for all those who might be interested in hearing about the proposed school. Hundreds of people attended each session. Registration was held for parishioners only on Saturday, February 3, 1996; nonparishioners were allowed to register the following Saturday. By the end of these two registration days, it was decided that there were sufficient students to open three kindergarten classes, two each of grades 1 to 6, one of grade 7, and one of grade 8. Waiting lists were immediately started in most grade levels.

While construction moved along at an amazing pace, teachers were interviewed and hired during the spring of 1996. Many of those hired were parishioners who had been working in government-sponsored (public) schools previously. Every effort was made to coordinate the hiring of staff and the acceptance of students with the pastors and principals of neighboring Catholic schools. The principal of Annunciation also offered to meet with the pastors of all neighboring parishes to keep them informed of the progress of Annunciation Catholic Academy.

Along with Father Caverly, Bill Orosz, chair of the advisory board, and Mark McLaughlin, director of operations for the parish, continued to oversee all aspects of the project. They also met regularly with the principal concerning staffing, the budget, and purchases of furniture, texts, and equipment. Since the school was to be highly technological—containing 110 totally networked computers, a centralized media retrieval system, an automated library, a closed-circuit television, and a state-of-the-art sound system—their expertise and guidance was essential in making all the pieces work together while dealing with several major vendors and providers and the architect and builder.

It is important to note that all decisions regarding technology were made based on educational goals and objectives. From the onset of the project, the principal had a vision of what could be achieved through the use of technology; the members of the advisory board were in agreement. Only teachers who would be comfortable in this highly technological school setting were hired, and ample opportunity for training was built into the budget and school schedule.

Construction of the building was completed in July, a month before schedule. A certificate of occupancy was obtained from the City of Altamonte Springs on July 17, 1996, and the office staff moved into the building on August 1, 1996.

Classes began for grades K through 8 on September 1, 1996, just 18 months after Father Caverly asked a small group of parishioners if they felt there was interest in starting a school!

St. Thomas Aquinas School

Diocese of Orlando, Florida

Maureen Huntington, Ed.S., Superintendent of Schools

The Diocese of Orlando was established June 16, 1968. In August of 1989, the first school in the diocese, St. Thomas Aquinas School, in St. Cloud, Florida, opened with 123 students in preschool through grade 2.

During the mid-1980s, the parishioners of St. Thomas Aquinas Parish became more and more anxious about the availability of a Catholic school education for their children. The closest Catholic schools were full and had long waiting lists, and parents found it difficult, if not impossible, to provide a Catholic school education for their children. After several successful building projects at the parish were completed, the pastor, Rev. Fabian Gimeno, promised the parents and parishioners a Catholic school.

Initially, discussions regarding a new school included members of a neighboring parish with ideas of a joint venture for both parishes. After much discussion, however, it was decided that each parish would build its own Catholic school in its own time frame. In the fall of 1988, Father Fabian and members of the St. Thomas Aquinas Parish met with the diocesan finance committee to review their plan for a school and gain the committee's support for a capital campaign. They also met with the building coordinator of the diocese to begin the feasibility study for the school. A fund-raising feasibility study was also initiated with the assistance of the diocesan development office.

During 1988 and into 1989, the superintendent of schools, Dr. Richard Fenchek, met with Father Fabian and members of the parish community to develop the concept of the school, the building design, the curriculum, and the governance structure of the school. During

1988, Sister Linda Martin, OSU, an Ursuline from Cleveland, Ohio, answered the invitation from Father Fabian to become principal and administer the new school. Sister Linda, while continuing to administer her own school in Ohio, began to work with Dr. Fenchek, Father Fabian and the parishioners of St. Thomas Aquinas, and the newly formed school board on the arduous tasks of fund-raising, program development, school board development, hiring, and registering new students.

The funding to build the school came from a parish capital campaign. The Diocese of Orlando requires that all projects have at least 50 percent of the cost of the project in cash on hand before any construction can begin. The other 50 percent can be borrowed from the diocesan internal bank to complete the project. To begin the capital campaign, large donations were solicited from members of the community. The pastor, in conjunction with his parish council and parents, developed a three-year pledge program to fund the initial phase of the school plant. The school was built in three phases, with the final phase being completed for the 1995-1996 school year.

In August of 1996, St. Thomas Aquinas School began its eighth year. It received its initial accreditation from the Florida Catholic Conference last school year, just several months before the first eighth-grade graduation occurred.

Since August of 1989, five more elementary schools have opened in the diocese, and each of them is a parish school. The building funds came from the parish community with assistance from the Diocese of Orlando. Each parish school began from the pastor's response to the needs of his parish community to have a Catholic school. The schools receive various types of additional financial support from the parish, ranging from operational support to the purchase of furnishings for new classrooms.

The three sections that follow illustrate the various steps the Diocese of Orlando Office of Schools followed before building the new parish schools. These sections are (1) Plan for Determining the Feasibility of Establishing Catholic Schools in the Diocese of Orlando, (2) Suggested Timeline for the Planning Process, and (3) Diocesan Review.

PLAN FOR DETERMINING THE FEASIBILITY OF ESTABLISHING CATHOLIC SCHOOLS IN THE DIOCESE OF ORLANDO

Assumptions

There is pressure from a number of sources to build new Catholic schools in the Diocese of Orlando. Policy analysts at the local and the diocesan levels need information to help them make decisions about new school facilities. Since new institutions will demand an annual input of resources, it is important that diocesan officials and local groups address the significant related issues that will arise. The more information that diocesan and local groups have during their decision making, the better informed their decisions will be. Although such information will not ensure the success of any new institution, the information-gathering process will help local and diocesan officials to clarify their own positions and to be more realistic in their goals and objectives.

What follows is a plan for gathering information relative to opening a new Catholic school. Policy analysts at the local and diocesan levels will be able to use the information to help them make initial decisions about the need for, and the feasibility of, such a school.

The plan is constructed to be operationalized at a certain point in the decision-making process. Basically, that point is when any parish has developed a serious intent to open a new Catholic school. Up to that point, it is assumed that a number of things have taken place:

1. Religious and lay leaders of the parish have met on several occasions to explore the possibility of opening a new school.

2. The pastor and the parish council have considered the question and decided to go ahead with the planning effort.

3. The parish leaders have contacted the diocesan superintendent of schools about the project and have requested assistance from the diocese to implement the planning process. The Office of Schools has agreed to support the parish in conducting the feasibility study.

At this point, the parish and the diocese are ready to put into operation the plan for the feasibility study contained herein.

Model Plan for Conducting a Feasibility Study

The parish itself must set up a structure for organizing and carrying out the feasibility study. Before too much time or effort is invested in detailed feasibility studies, however, the pastor and the parish council should conduct an interest investigation using a short survey such as that found in Exhibit 7 at the end of this chapter. The purpose of the survey is to determine the interest of the parishioners in operating a parish school. If the results of this preliminary survey indicate substantial interest and support, then the next steps of the process should be implemented.

We suggest the parish establish a feasibility study committee composed of 9 to 12 members representative of various groups and points of view in the parish. If necessary, the committee may be assisted by one or more subcommittees assigned to conduct the individual studies that will be considered by the committee in reaching its conclusions.

Once the feasibility study committee is formed, it needs a plan to complete the study. A suggested decision-making process is given in Exhibit 8 at the end of this chapter. This timeline summarizes the actions of the study committee and indicates several termination points of the study should the feedback become negative.

Feasibility Study Committee: Roles and Responsibilities

This group of 9 to 12 members may be appointed by the pastor and parish council or be selected in some other manner. Its responsibilities are to identify the goals and objectives for a new parochial school. The feasibility study committee oversees the entire process once the interest survey of the parish council shows support for a school. This committee also drafts the final report to the diocese through the parish council.

The feasibility study committee should consider and follow the procedures below, as appropriate for the local situation. (See Exhibit 9 at the end of this chapter for a sample outline of the study.)

- Identify the educational goals and objectives of the parish and publish them widely.
- Hold formal and informal meetings in the parish community regarding the goals and objectives, modifying these where needed.
- Study needed elements for starting a school, establishing sub-committees if necessary.
- Meet with the pastor and the parish council periodically to report on the progress of the study and to decide whether to stop the process or continue. The committee may want to involve diocesan officials in these decisions.
- Draft a final report for presentation to the parish council, pastor, parishioners, and diocesan officials after council approval.

A. Demographic Study. The purpose of this study is to collect and integrate the data on the potential population of children for the proposed parish elementary school. To accomplish this task, some or all of these procedures should be followed:

1. Collect such data as parish population, number of school-age children in the parish, transiency, baptisms, and public-school enrollment trends.

38

    2. Gather data on parish and community population projections, growth and decline patterns, and proposed housing developments.

    3. Examine the transportation possibilities and potential problems.

    4. Collect data on the availability of community support systems, such as libraries, parks, and recreation centers.

    5. Seek assistance from local public-school districts in compiling data on past, present, and future school-age population trends.

    6. Get commitments in writing, by name and family, from those who would send children to the school.

    7. Study data from other diocesan parochial schools on such items as class size, minimum numbers of pupils needed to operate a school, adult-to-student ratios, and faculty-to-student ratios.

    8. Study the impact that opening a new parochial school could have on existing parochial schools that enroll children from the parish.

    B. Educational Program Study. The purpose of this study is to design an educational organization plan (i.e., grade levels) and program of studies consistent with the overall goals and objectives established by the feasibility study committee. To accomplish this task, some of the following should be accomplished:

    1. Review the goals and objectives of the parish and diocese.

    2. Examine the alternative organizational plans in the diocese and in the surrounding public-school district(s); for example, preschool through grade 8, kindergarten through grade 8, and kindergarten through grade 6 are some of the many organizational schemes possible.

    3. Develop an overall educational program of studies, using the diocesan and state department of education curriculum requirements as guidelines; for example, How will subjects like art, music, and physical education be incorporated into the school? Will there be special programs in reading or speech?

    4. Plan for the harmonious transition from the parish school to other schools, both Catholic and public.

    Exhibit 13 at the end of this chapter provides a sample form for estimating instructional supplies and equipment costs for a five-year period.

    C. Personnel Study. The purpose of this study is to determine the personnel needs for beginning a parish school based on the organizational plan and program of studies recommended in the educational program study. To accomplish its task, the committee should consider doing the following:

    1. Study the educational philosophy, the organizational plan(s), and the program of studies recommended.

    2. Determine the number of people needed in the following categories to implement the above plans:
- Teaching personnel
- Administrative personnel
- Support personnel (secretarial, custodial)

    3. Determine the personnel resource expectations from the parish and community:
- Public school assistants through special categorical aid, such as Title I aides, reading specialists, and psychologists
- Volunteer assistants—parents, senior citizens
- Others, such as high school tutors, student aides from universities

    4. Attempt to secure a commitment from a religious order, if desired.

    5. Project personnel needs for a three- to five-year period, especially if the school will not be fully operational in the first year or two.

    6. Compare personnel data collection with diocesan information and standards.

Exhibit 14 at the end of this chapter provides a sample form for estimating personnel costs.

    D. Building Study. The purpose of this study is to determine where a new school building will be built or what existing facility or facilities may be used to operate an elementary school. To accomplish this task, some or all of the items below should be considered.

    1. Study the goals, objectives, recommended organizational plan, and personnel and population data.

    2. Investigate existing school-site resources and opportunities to use them.

    3. Investigate new-school site availability and costs.

    4. Meet with diocesan and public school officials regarding new or existing buildings and grounds.

    5. Study state and local regulations and codes regarding schools.

    6. Evaluate the use and availability of existing facilities and what modifications would be needed in those facilities.

7. Prepare a report that includes:
- Site selection
- Building plan or modifications to existing structures
- Plant maintenance and operating cost estimates
- Equipment needed in the school
- Start-up costs for the building

Exhibits 10 through 13 at the end of this chapter are sample forms that may be helpful to the committee in carrying out these tasks.

E. Financial Study. The purpose of this study is twofold: (a) to determine the costs of establishing the parish school and (b) to study the potential revenue sources. To accomplish these tasks, the committee should:

1. Study the other reports and determine their financial impact.
- Estimate the personnel expenses of the school.
- Estimate the other operating expenses.
- Estimate the capital expenses.

2. Determine the costs for the start-up year and for the third and fifth years.

3. Determine the per-pupil expenditure for the first year.

4. Determine the tuition rate for the first year.

5. Determine the amount of parish subsidy needed the first year.

6. Estimate the parish's ability to raise the capital for the building program and its ability to contribute to the yearly operation of the school.

7. Compare the income and expense figures of the school with those of existing schools in the diocese, especially those schools in the upper quartile of expenses.

At the end of this chapter, Exhibit 9, item X may be helpful for estimating income.

SUGGESTED TIMELINE FOR THE PLANNING PROCESS

The timeline suggested in Exhibit 8 at the end of this chapter represents realistic estimates of what needs to be studied and how much time volunteers will need to provide to carry out the committee tasks. The timeline also suggests that the feasibility study committee spend the first month carrying out the tasks listed and that each study be given an allotted amount of time in the planning process. We suggest about 4.5 months for the demographic study, 4 months for the educational program study, 3 months for the personnel study, 4 months for the building study, 5 months for the financial study, and a total of 3 months for preparation of the final report, meetings, and the final presentation. This timeline may have to be modified to meet specific needs and interests.

Usually, community interest in creating a Catholic elementary school is originated or developed by the local parish council. The parish council determines the general, but not the special, interests of the Catholic community it serves regarding the establishment of a Catholic elementary school. For this reason, we recommend that the parish council, in the preliminary stages of this feasibility study, initiate a method of soliciting parent-parishioner interest. A sample survey form for investigating this interest is provided in Exhibit 7 at the end of this chapter.

The results of the interest survey and of preliminary discussions with some members of the power structure of the parish and community will suggest to the council whether or not it should proceed with a feasibility study. If the council decides to proceed, the format suggested in Exhibit 9 at the end of this chapter is applicable and the timeline suggested in Exhibit 8 is warranted.

The feasibility study committee should use the cost projection sheets found in Exhibits 10 through 14. The cost projection sheets are illustrative and not all-inclusive; however, they are designed to assist the committee to get an idea of the items that must be considered in estimating and projecting costs.

It becomes obvious upon examining the tasks of the feasibility study committee that the overall coordination of this effort is essential. The studies cannot be conducted in isolation. Thus, the foremost responsibility of the study committee is to see that all tasks are accomplished within specified time constraints and established priorities. Regular accountability in performing the assigned tasks should be insisted upon by the study committee.

Once the reports have been written, the feasibility study committee needs to analyze the report data and recommendations in order to decide if a new school is feasible. If affirmative, the last steps in Exhibit 9 at the end of this chapter should then be implemented.

1. The feasibility study committee prepares its initial report stating its decision, interpreting or altering the major information and recommendations of each study.

2. The report is distributed to the parishioners, the pastor, and the parish council.

3. Public meetings are held to obtain feedback and answer questions.

4. The pastor and parish council provide feedback and suggestions.

5. The feasibility study committee prepares a final draft report stating that a new school is or is not feasible.

6. The report is presented to the parish council and the parish.

7. The parish council approves the plan for operating a parish school, disapproves the plan, or requires additional information before making a final decision.

If the parish council approves the feasibility study committee's report, the next steps in the process are a review by the diocese and a decision concerning opening the school.

Interest-Investigation Survey

The intent of the interest-investigation survey is to use it, with appropriate modifications specific to an individual parish, as a way of informing the pastor and the parish council about parishioners' general support for, and interest in, starting a school. Should the responses warrant further study on the costs, site acquisition, tuition, etc., then the parish council should appoint a study committee and spend the time and money on the planning details. If there is no general interest and support, then there is no need to proceed beyond analyzing the data generated by this instrument. See Exhibit 7 at the end of this chapter for a sample of the instrument.

DIOCESAN REVIEW

In preparing for the presentation of its proposal to diocesan officials and the diocesan school board, the parish should consider whether or not it has addressed fully the following questions:

A. Feasibility Study Committee
1. Has the group formulated written goals and objectives?
2. Are the goals and objectives clear and consistent with the overall educational mission of the diocese and the Catholic Church?
3. Has a parish interest-investigation survey been conducted?
4. Does the survey reflect a representative sample of the parish community?
5. Does the survey reflect a wide range of support for a new school?

6. What percentage of the survey sample states unqualified support for, and interest in, a new school? Is this percentage large enough to warrant building a new school?
7. What kind of support is there from the pastor and the parish council at this stage?

B. Demographic Study
   1. Has the committee collected current figures for the parish and the community?
   2. What are the current population figures for the parish and the community?
      a. Are there enough families in the parish to support a school?
      b. Are there enough families with school-age children to provide a steady core of students for the school? If not, will the school be able to draw students from nearby parishes?
      c. What effect will opening a new school have on existing Catholic and public schools?
   3. Have comparisons of data been made regarding income and expenses of schools in parishes in the highest quartile of expenditures in the diocese?
   4. Has the committee identified community support systems in its report?
   5. How will identified transportation and traffic problems affect the continued operation of the school?
   6. What other information is presented to show that the school will be operational over a long period of time?

C. Educational Program Study
   1. Is the proposed educational organization plan consistent with the goals and objectives of the parish and with the philosophy and goals of the diocese?
   2. Is the organization plan appropriate for the kind of educational program proposed?
   3. Will the educational plan meet diocesan requirements for curriculum and time schedules?
   4. How does the parish mesh with educational organizations in the community? Will there be smooth transitions to other schools?

D. Personnel Study
  1. What has the committee done about staffing the school with religious and lay teachers?
  2. Are the personnel projections realistic and consistent with the educational program and organizational plans?
  3. Are personnel resources consistent with diocesan policies and with comparable parochial schools?
  4. Does the report include adequate provisions for support personnel?
  5. Are there contingency provisions for increasing or reducing personnel depending on student enrollment?
  6. What information is presented showing anticipated support from the local public-school districts and community agencies?

E. Building Study
  1. Are school building plans adequate to meet the goals and educational plans provided by the other committees?
  2. Is the proposed site or existing building accessible and available for use?
  3. Does the committee report include equipment needs, facility expansion, and cost projections?
  4. Has the committee explored state and local codes for school construction and operation?

F. Financial Study
  1. Has the committee provided adequate data on which to make a feasibility decision?
  2. Using diocesan data, how does the financial picture of the school compare with existing Catholic schools?
     a. What will the per-pupil expenditure be?
     b. What will the tuition scale be?
     c. What will the parish subsidy be?
     d. What outside fund-raising will be needed in order to operate a school?
  3. What is the plan to raise the capital for constructing a new school or converting an existing building?
  4. Are the cost projections realistic?
  5. What effect will these plans have on the total indebtedness of the parish?
  6. Is the projected tuition affordable for the families most likely to send children to the school?

7. Does the report demonstrate the ability of the parish to meet construction costs and operational costs over a three- to five-year period?

G. Final Tasks of the Feasibility Study Committee
   1. Has the committee widely distributed its report, solicited suggestions, held meetings of parishioners, and drafted a final report?
   2. Were the recommendations of the committee accepted by the pastor and the parish council?
   3. Is there unanimity on the desirability and feasibility of operating a parish school?

Exhibit 7

Sample Interest-Investigation Survey

Dear Parishioners of _____ Parish:

The parish council, in cooperation with our pastor, is trying to determine the attitudes of the people of the parish toward the establishment of a parish elementary school. We are asking each family in the parish and each single person not living with his/her family to complete this brief questionnaire and leave it with a member of the committee today.

Before the committee goes any further with its plans, a determination has to be made about the advisability of starting a school and about who would be willing and able to support such a school. Please be as accurate as possible in your responses, and answer all questions that are appropriate to you.

We thank you in advance for your cooperation. God bless you.

Joe Smith, Chairman
Parish Council

1. What is your present family status? (Check one)
   _____ Single
   _____ Widow/widower
   _____ Married, no children at home
   _____ Married with children at home
   _____ Single parent
   _____ Other (Explain) _____

2. If you have children at home, please list the sex, date of birth, grade level, and present school of each of your children.

Sex	Birthdate	Grade	Present School
_____	_____	_____	_____
_____	_____	_____	_____
_____	_____	_____	_____
_____	_____	_____	_____
_____	_____	_____	_____
_____	_____	_____	_____
_____	_____	_____	_____

3. Do you feel this parish should proceed with plans to open a parish elementary school?

                  Yes_____   No_____   Not sure _____

4. If the parish decided to open a school, would you be willing to:
   a. Contribute to a building fund?

                     Yes_____   No_____   Not sure _____

   b. Assist in fund-raising efforts?

                     Yes_____   No_____   Not sure _____

   c. Send some or all of your children to the school (if applicable)?

                     Yes_____   No_____   Not sure _____

   d. Serve on a committee to help plan the school?

                     Yes_____   No_____   Not sure _____

   e. Donate time to help construct the school or school ground?

                     Yes_____   No_____   Not sure _____

5. If you have elementary school-age children who might attend the parish school:
   a. Are you willing to pay a tuition of about $_____ per child?

                     Yes_____   No_____   Not sure _____

   b. Would you send your children to more than one elementary school (split register)?

                     Yes_____   No_____   Not sure _____

Check the grade level(s) of your children most likely to attend the parish school next year.

___K   ___1   ___2   ___3   ___4   ___5   ___6   ___7   ___8

6. Please make any comments or suggestions on the back of this page.

Exhibit 8

Suggested Timeline for Feasibility Study Committee

MONTH 1
Feasibility study committee meets to—
- Discuss purposes, objectives, tasks, and the educational organization
- Decide on planning model and timeline
- Determine other meeting dates during the first month
- Answer questions, clarify tasks, etc., offered by committee members
- Set schedule, timelines, etc.
- Initiate the demographic study

MONTHS 2-5
Committee meets to—
- Discuss tasks for the demographic study
- Determine methods for accomplishing the tasks
- Establish data collection procedures
- Determine adequacy of timeline, establish meeting dates, etc.
- Obtain commitments from families of potential students
- Collect information concerning population trends from government and diocesan sources
- Analyze the data
- Write the report on data and family commitments
- Discuss the demographic report and decide whether the data suggest proceeding with the study
- Activate the educational program, personnel, and building studies

MONTHS 3-9
Committee meets to—
- Discuss tasks for the educational program study
- Determine methods for accomplishing the tasks
- Establish time schedule and data collection procedures
- Develop cost projections for the school's educational program (See Exhibit 13)

Committee meets to—
- Discuss tasks for the personnel study
- Determine methods for accomplishing the tasks

- Establish time schedule and data collection procedures
- Develop cost projections for the school's personnel (See Exhibit 14)

Committee meets to—

- Discuss tasks for the building study
- Determine methods for accomplishing the tasks
- Establish time schedule and data collection procedures
- Develop cost projections for the school building and grounds (See Exhibits 10 and 11)

Feasibility study committee meets to—

- Review all reports and recommendations to date
- Initiate the financial study

Committee meets to—

- Discuss tasks for the financial study
- Determine methods for accomplishing the tasks
- Establish time schedule and data collection procedures
- Develop income projections and consolidate cost projections
- Analyze the impact of a new school on the parish budget

MONTHS 10-12

Feasibility study committee meets to—

- Decide on procedures for collecting all reports and recommendations
- Discuss recommendations and prepare the final report

Feasibility study committee—

- Disseminates preliminary report, holds one or more public meetings, and holds small-group meetings with the pastor, parish council, and community leaders
- Prepares the final report and disseminates it to parish groups
- Meets with diocesan officials and the diocesan school board to discuss the final report and answer questions regarding data and recommendations in the report

The diocesan officials and board meet to discuss the report and the meeting with the feasibility study committee.

The diocesan school board announces its decision.

Exhibit 9

Sample Format for Feasibility Study for Catholic Schools

   I.   Area: Description of the proposed area to be served

  II.   Population
- A. Total population of the area to be served
- B. Ethnic/racial characteristics (totals)
  1. White/non-Hispanic
  2. Hispanic
  3. Black/non-Hispanic
  4. Asian
  5. Native American
  6. Other
- C. Total children in the area by grade level
  1. Preschool (ages birth to kindergarten)
  2. Grades 1-8
  3. Grades 9-12
- D. Brief description of the planned growth of the area to be served

 III.   Feeder parishes
- A. Identification/description of the feeder parishes
- B. Number of families registered in each feeder parish
- C. Number of families registered in each parish who regularly support the parish
- D. Total of Catholic students in grades 1-8 in each parish
- E. Total of Catholic students in grades 9-12 in each parish
- F. Total of students attending Catholic schools in the service areas by grade level
  1. Prekindergarten
  2. Kindergarten
  3. Grades 1-8
  4. Grades 9-12

 IV.   Proposed student population
- A. Total proposed student population
- B. Number of students from each parish
- C. Grades
- D. Number of students in each grade
- E. Ethnic/racial characteristics of students in proposed population (totals)

        1. White/non-Hispanic
        2. Hispanic
        3. Black/non-Hispanic
        4. Asian
        5. Native American
        6. Other

    F. Socioeconomic characteristics of parent(s) of proposed student population (approximates)
        1. Professionals
        2. Nonprofessionals
        3. Income distribution
           a. $40,000 or more
           b. $30,000-$39,999
           c. $20,000 to $29,999
           d. Under $20,000

V. Personnel
    A. Number of diocesan priests available for positions
        1. Administration
        2. Teaching
    B. Number of religious priests available for positions
        1. Administration
        2. Teaching
    C. Number of religious sisters available for positions
        1. Administration
        2. Teaching
    D. Number of religious brothers available for positions
        1. Administration
        2. Teaching

VI. Boards
    A. Development board
        1. Should one be organized?
        2. If so, what should be its composition?
        3. What should be its responsibilities?
        4. What agency should oversee finances?
    B. School board
        1. What type is desirable?
        2. What should be its representation?

VII. Positive and negative factors
    A. Resources within the area that would support the proposed development
    B. Factors that would hinder the proposal

VIII. Alternative sites: Description of possible alternative sites and positive and negative factors of each alternative

IX. Budget
  A. Capital costs
    1. Site construction
    2. Equipment
       Total
  B. Operating costs (annual)
    1. Salaries
       a. Teachers
       b. Staff
    2. Employee benefits
    3. Contract services
    4. Materials/supplies
    5. Utilities
    6. School upkeep
    7. Depreciation
    8. Other (specify)
       Total

X. Revenue sources
  A. Capital costs
    1. Sources of revenue and amount from each, including parishes, individuals, grants, foundations, trusts, and corporations
    2. Collection plan in time frames
  B. Operating costs
    1. Possibilities of establishing an endowment fund to assist operational expenses
    2. Tuition per child (scale) and total revenue from tuition
  C. Other sources and total

XI. Deficit: Assessment of each feeder parish's ability to pay a fair share of a capital or operating deficit

XII. Cost-effectiveness analysis: Investment in relation to projected benefits

XIII. Persons responsible for the project at local level (pastors and laypeople)
  A. Name
  B. Address
  C. Telephone number(s)
  D. Parish

Exhibit 10

Cost Projections: Building

1. New Construction Costs	Number	Estimate*
a. Classrooms	_____	_____
b. Auditorium/multipurpose room	_____	_____
c. Cafeteria/lunch room	_____	_____
d. Gymnasium/multipurpose room	_____	_____
e. Health care room	_____	_____
f. Heating/ventilation	_____	_____
g. Administrative office(s)	_____	_____
h. Permits/fees	_____	_____
i. Other (specify) _____	_____	_____
Totals	_____	_____

2. Remodeling Costs for Parishes with Existing Facilities		
a. Classrooms	_____	_____
b. Auditorium/multipurpose room	_____	_____
c. Cafeteria/lunch room	_____	_____
d. Gymnasium/multipurpose room	_____	_____
e. Health care room	_____	_____
f. Heating/ventilation	_____	_____
g. Administrative office(s)	_____	_____
h. Permits/fees	_____	_____
i. Other (specify) _____	_____	_____
Totals	_____	_____

Estimates should be based on the studies of the building and finance committees.

Exhibit 11

Cost Projections - Five-Year Plan: Elementary School Operations

Expense	Year 1	Year 2	Year 3	Year 4	Year 5
Boilers					
Pumps					
Fuel					
Electrical fixtures					
Utilities					
Toilets/sinks					
Showers					
Telephones					
Contract services					
Repairs					
Maintenance plan					
Replacement costs					
Furniture - office					
Equipment - office					
Convent rental					
Convent equipment					
Convent supplies					
Convent insurance					
Auto purchase					
Auto insurance					
Cafeteria equipment					
Cafeteria supplies					
Custodial equipment					
Custodial supplies					
Property insurance					
Student insurance					
Totals					

Exhibit 12

Cost Projections - Five-Year Plan:
Elementary School Grounds

Expense	Year 1	Year 2	Year 3	Year 4	Year 5
Playground equipment	_____	_____	_____	_____	_____
Playground supplies	_____	_____	_____	_____	_____
Ground equipment	_____	_____	_____	_____	_____
Curbs/gutters	_____	_____	_____	_____	_____
Driveways	_____	_____	_____	_____	_____
Sidewalks	_____	_____	_____	_____	_____
Parking lot	_____	_____	_____	_____	_____
Water/gas meters	_____	_____	_____	_____	_____
Fences/gates	_____	_____	_____	_____	_____
Bicycle racks	_____	_____	_____	_____	_____
Turf - lawns	_____	_____	_____	_____	_____
Trees - shrubs	_____	_____	_____	_____	_____
Sprinkling system	_____	_____	_____	_____	_____
Drainage	_____	_____	_____	_____	_____
Other (specify)	_____	_____	_____	_____	_____
Other (specify)	_____	_____	_____	_____	_____
Totals	_____	_____	_____	_____	_____

Explanations: _____

_____

_____

_____

_____

Exhibit 13

Cost Projections - Five-Year Plan:
Elementary School Instructional Supplies/Equipment

Expense	Year 1	Year 2	Year 3	Year 4	Year 5
Textbooks:					
Reading	___	___	___	___	___
Math	___	___	___	___	___
Science	___	___	___	___	___
Social studies	___	___	___	___	___
Spelling	___	___	___	___	___
Other (specify)	___	___	___	___	___
Other (specify)	___	___	___	___	___
Workbooks:					
Reading	___	___	___	___	___
Math	___	___	___	___	___
Science	___	___	___	___	___
Social studies	___	___	___	___	___
Spelling	___	___	___	___	___
Other (specify)	___	___	___	___	___
Library	___	___	___	___	___
Library reference books	___	___	___	___	___
Teaching supplies	___	___	___	___	___
A-V supplies	___	___	___	___	___
A-V equipment	___	___	___	___	___
Office supplies	___	___	___	___	___
Office equipment	___	___	___	___	___
Classroom supplies	___	___	___	___	___
Classroom equipment	___	___	___	___	___
Classroom	___	___	___	___	___

(continued)

	Year 1	Year 2	Year 3	Year 4	Year 5
Custodial supplies	_____	_____	_____	_____	_____
Custodial equipment	_____	_____	_____	_____	_____
Cabinets/hardware	_____	_____	_____	_____	_____
Shelving	_____	_____	_____	_____	_____
Bookcases	_____	_____	_____	_____	_____
Shades/blinds	_____	_____	_____	_____	_____
Intercom/fire alarm	_____	_____	_____	_____	_____
Lockers	_____	_____	_____	_____	_____
Physical education supplies	_____	_____	_____	_____	_____
Physical education equipment	_____	_____	_____	_____	_____
Bulletin and chalk-boards	_____	_____	_____	_____	_____
Science equipment	_____	_____	_____	_____	_____
Extracurricular equipment	_____	_____	_____	_____	_____
Extracurricular supplies	_____	_____	_____	_____	_____
Other	_____	_____	_____	_____	_____
Other	_____	_____	_____	_____	_____
Totals	_____	_____	_____	_____	_____

Explanations: _____

_____

_____

_____

Exhibit 14

Cost Projections - Five-Year Plan:
Elementary School Personnel

Expense	Year 1	Year 2	Year 3	Year 4	Year 5
Salaries:					
Principal					
Lay teachers					
Religious teachers					
Substitute teachers (estimated total)					
Secretary					
Custodian					
Food Service					
Benefits:					
Social Security (exc. employee's share)					
Fringe benefits					
Unemployment compensation					
Teacher in-service					
Other (specify)					
Other (specify)					
Totals					

Explanations: _____

_____

_____

_____

59

St. Francis Middle School: A Three-Parish Middle School

Diocese of Sacramento, California

Raymond L. John, Ed.D., Principal

S t. Francis Middle School in Palo Cedro, California, opened in August 1994. It served two classes each of sixth-, seventh-, and eighth-graders. Today, there are 132 students at the school, with an anticipated enrollment of 150-160 for the 1997-1998 school year.

The need for St. Francis Middle School came about because Shasta County is one of the fastest-growing regions in the nation. The two local Catholic schools, St. Joseph in Redding and Sacred Heart in Anderson, were operating at capacity and had waiting lists of families. In addition to the Catholic students, a lot of non-Catholic children wanted to come to the county's only two Catholic schools.

A long-range plan survey was sent out in 1993 to determine the need for more Catholic schools. The results clearly showed overwhelming support for a middle school and a high school.

By chance, an existing private school closed and was up for sale. The purchase price was $2.7 million for 22 classrooms, an administrative building, and a gymnasium (with a chapel and music room in it) on 40 acres. The Diocese of Sacramento purchased the property at this incredible price, with the condition that St. Joseph Parish and Our Lady of Mercy Parish in Redding and Sacred Heart Parish in Anderson would launch a large capital campaign drive to pay for the property and the future buildings. The community responded beautifully, and the campaign has brought in over $1 million since its beginning in 1994. After the first campaign is completed, a second campaign will begin to complete the campus.

Today, the school has full spiritual, academic, and athletic programs under the direction of three local pastors and their appointed principal. The academic program involves a seven-period day with all basic subjects (religion, math, English, social studies, science, and physical education) and several electives (band, choral group, fine arts, computers, and study skills). Recent standardized tests show the students are above the national average in all subjects.

Besides the physical education program, there is an extensive sports program. The students compete in soccer, basketball, baseball, softball, volleyball, cross country, and track. All students are encouraged to participate, and coaches are chosen for their ability to teach rather than to win.

The governance structure has improved a lot since 1994. Instead of one head pastor, all three pastors work together to advise the principal. Bit by bit, the parishes of St. Joseph, Sacred Heart, and Our Lady of Mercy are viewing St. Francis Middle School as their "parish" school.

The future of the school looks great. Plans are under way to build a new middle-school building and to leave the present school building as the high school.

Since I am the principal of St. Francis Middle School and of Bishop Quinn High School, I will save my recommendations for things to do when opening a new school until the next chapter, on Bishop Quinn High School.

Bishop Quinn High School

Diocese of Sacramento, California

Raymond L. John, Ed.D., Principal

Bishop Quinn High School opened in Palo Cedro, California, in August 1995. It served a freshman class of 26 students. Today, there are 63 freshmen and sophomores, with an anticipated enrollment of 110 for the 1997-1998 school year. The first graduation class will be the class of 1999, at which point the enrollment will be around 150. Without a single Catholic high school in the entire county, Shasta County had needed such a school for over 20 years. Many Catholic families had hoped to have their children go on to a Catholic high school after completing their Catholic elementary school. As the need arose, an incredible opportunity occurred. An existing private school closed and put the entire plant up for sale. For $2.7 million, the Diocese of Sacramento purchased 22 classrooms, an administrative building, and a gymnasium (with a chapel and music room in it) on 40 acres.

With the need for a middle school and a high school, the county saw the available plant as a godsend. Since 1995, the entire plant has been thoroughly renovated, including painting of the interior and exterior, landscaping, re-roofing, and construction of playing fields. Currently, the two schools are sharing the same facilities until the new middle school is built on the property. A campaign is under way to complete the project (see the preceding chapter on St. Francis Middle School).

Bishop Quinn High School, although small, has already made a significant impact in Shasta County. Students, for example, have been honored by the local Rotary, Veterans of Foreign War, Knights of Columbus, and our congressman, Representative Wally Herger.

Each quarter, the students prepare and present to the administration a portfolio of their spiritual, academic, and athletic accomplishments. At semester, they take seven 2-hour exams and then present their portfolios in an oral presentation to the faculty. In 1999, the first senior class will take senior orals.

The school's spiritual program involves religion instruction, masses, liturgies, Christian community service, and community involvement. Many of the students work at Mercy Medical Hospital, the Northern Valley Catholic Social Services second-hand store, and the local museum, for example.

The academic program has the portfolio as its main thrust. The curriculum is college preparatory in all subjects—classes are taught either as college prep or as honors classes. Despite its small size, Bishop Quinn High School has a student government, a band, a choral group, drama, fine arts, a computer group, a yearbook, and clubs.

The athletic program is a full one. This year, we have girls' volleyball, boys' and girls' basketball, football, baseball, softball in league competition, and tennis and golf as club sports. In only our second year of sports, the girls won the league championship in volleyball.

The field-trips program has included overnighters to San Francisco for the theater, the Pacific Ocean for camping, snow trips, and museum trips.

Overall, Bishop Quinn High School has grown dramatically in its first year. Although the school is small, the students often say it is run and operated like a school of 500. The advantage with the size is that we all have become a family, and we look forward to June 1999, when the first graduates will leave school as strong Catholic leaders for the future.

Recommendations for Opening a New Catholic School

In the preceding chapter and earlier in this one, I discussed St. Francis Middle School and Bishop Quinn High School. Both are doing well and will continue to get better.

In looking back, I would recommend people consider doing the following when opening a school:

1. Carefully work with the county and city governments when purchasing the property. The "site-use" permit for the school was immediately canceled upon the sale of the property. When we bought it, we had to apply for a new site-use permit. We are still trying to get

it two years later, because the county has attached 71 conditions to be met before the permit can be granted.

2. Be realistic, not optimistic, with your projections. Because everyone was excited, they predicted population numbers for the school far below the eventual reality. This cost us dollars, since the county based its sewer assessment on our population figures. The capital campaign was another example where people expected much more money coming in than actually did.

3. Keep the committees to a minimum. Coming in as a principal was very difficult for me. People in committees had been working so long and hard on philosophy, curriculum, site maintenance, long-range plans, etc., that it was difficult to let them know that a college-prep curriculum set up for 500 students does not necessarily work with 26 students and 2 teachers. My advice is to do some committee work but not to get so specific that the new administrator is hampered.

4. Tell your story and tell it often. I found that many people felt out of the loop because they were not informed often enough of the progress of the middle school or high school. On a regular basis— through newsletters, parish bulletins, the press—let everyone know the progress you are making. False rumors about problems caused more pain than the real problems caused.

5. Call, call, call. There are a lot of Catholic schools opening throughout the country. Call several schools and ask very specific questions about what you should and should not do. You need to hear their stories—good and bad. Those of us who are going through this would love to help others to not make some of the mistakes we have made.

6. Pray. It sounds so simple, but it works. Sometimes I wake up and I am thoroughly overwhelmed with my jobs—principal of a new high school, principal of a new middle school, site-manager, director of a capital campaign, future-buildings coordinator, and public relations director for both schools. I then stop and remind myself of why I am here and why I chose to spend my life in Catholic education. My prayer is simple: "Lord, for whatever reason, you chose me for this awesome task. I don't know what was on your mind that day, but I accept your decision. But please be here with me each step of the way today. I'm scared. Thanks."

Back in 1969 when I started in Catholic schools, I kept hearing about all the schools that were closing. Little did I realize I would be finishing my career by opening two new schools. It is the highest honor I have had in my career. I congratulate each of you who are starting a new Catholic school or are even thinking about it. You are special people. My prayers are with you.

Checklist for Opening a New School

- Survey the entire community to determine need.
- Whether building or buying, know exactly what the city and county regulations are.
- Estimate four to five years of budgets with guaranteed subsidy.
- Estimate start-up costs (e.g., desks, chalkboards, books, paper, etc.).
- Hire the administrator at least six months before opening day.
- Have a transition committee between the school planners and those who actually open the school.
- Hire experienced teachers, since they can handle the constant change and uncertainty of a new school.
- Provide plenty of extracurricular activities to attract incoming students.
- Plan a large public relations campaign involving television, radio, newspapers, church bulletins, etc.
- Keep a list of every supporter, and make sure everyone gets thanked personally.
- Keep your sense of humor at all times.

Mary of Nazareth Catholic Elementary School

Archdiocese of Washington, D.C.

Sr. Frances Stavalo, MFP, M.A., Principal

Mary of Nazareth Catholic Elementary School was the dream of His Eminence James Cardinal Hickey, archbishop of Washington. Under his leadership, the archdiocese brought together seven parishes in the upper Montgomery County, Maryland, area to make a commitment to the school. The seven parishes included St. Paul, Damascus; St. Mary Church and Shrine, Barnesville; Mother Seton, Germantown; Sr. Rose of Lima, Gaithersburg; St. John Neumann, Gaithersburg; Our Lady of the Visitation, Darnestown; and Our Lady of the Presentation, Poolesville.

The archdiocese agreed to put forth the money needed to buy the land, begin the building process, and furnish the school. Msgr. Thomas Kane, from St. Patrick's Parish in Rockville, was chosen to oversee the project, in conjunction with the seven pastors or their appointed emissaries.

A search committee found land in the Darnestown area of upper Montgomery County. The property contained 189 acres and was the site of an existing building that was once a residential school. Also on the property was a large house, a garage, a storage barn, and a barn structure that had contained classrooms for the former school. The archdiocese purchased the land and its buildings for use by the school and for the Our Lady of the Visitation Parish. The brick building that housed the dormitory, library, and a few classrooms would be converted into living quarters for the religious teachers who were to come to the school. The new school building would be built off of this building. The barn structure would be modified to house four classrooms, two small offices, and a restroom facility. The school would begin its first year in this modest building.

In the meantime, surveys were sent out to the parishioners of the seven sponsoring parishes. Parents were asked if they were interested in enrolling their children in a new Catholic school and what grade or grades they were interested in. No other information was requested—this would not come until later. Letters were sent to the families who expressed interest in the school, and meetings were held to provide the parents with additional information.

It was decided that the school would grow by one grade level each year, up to the eighth grade. The school opened in the fall of 1994 with 86 students in kindergarten through grade 3.

For the second year, two rooms were utilized in the existing brick structure that housed the religious teachers. For the 1995 school year, the first-grade and fourth-grade students would be housed in this building, while the kindergarten, second, and third grades remained in the barn structure.

After a long delay in obtaining county permits, the construction crew started on the new school building, which would be attached to the existing brick structure. Initially estimated at $2.5 million, the final figures for construction and furnishing the new school came in at $3 million. Originally scheduled to open in January 1966, the new building was not ready until just before the start of the 1996-1997 school year. As late as August 1996, construction crews labored to finish the multipurpose room and the kitchen and to repair the heating/cooling system that had developed problems during the summer. A problem that was realized after the start of the school was the limited number of people allowed within the multipurpose room at one time. With a total capacity of only 180, set by the fire marshall, the room will not be able to be used for full-school functions once the school is at capacity.

After two long years, Mary of Nazareth School and its 183 students and teachers are now housed in their beautiful new building. The classrooms are large and commodious. Each room contains lockers for the students to use for their personal belongings. The school features a spacious front office, teachers' lounge, computer room, science lab, and health room. A library and day-care area are housed in the original brick building along with living quarters for the two religious orders who work and live at the school. Currently, six religious personnel and four lay teachers are employed at the school.

At its completion, the new structure cost $3 million for construction and furnishings. The school is paying for this mortgage with a cost-based tuition system. When the school opened in 1994, the tuition was $2,800 per student, with no family discounts and a textbook/materials fee of $200. This tuition was held through the 1995 school year. An increase to $3,000 occurred in 1996-1997, with a textbook fee of $300. This increase was initiated for two reasons: to cover the impending mortgage payments and because no increase had occurred in the previous year.

With much fanfare, the school was blessed and dedicated by the archbishop of Washington, James Cardinal Hickey, on September 28, 1996. Signs decorated the school ground and hallways, declaring "Your Dream...Our School. Thank you, Cardinal Hickey." The school library was dedicated to Cardinal Hickey and a plaque was installed for all to see. The first Catholic elementary school to open in the Montgomery County area in 30 years was now a reality.

In the years ahead, the school hopes to build a gymnasium, open a prekindergarten class, and possibly expand to double classrooms for each grade level.